Paving
Your Path to
POLICING

THE REALITY OF RECRUITMENT

by
Jeffrey H. Lurie

**PAVING
YOUR PATH**
PUBLISHING

Printed in the United States of America

10   9   8   7   6   5   4   3   2   1

ISBN: 0692378588

ISBN 13: 9780692378588

Library of Congress Control Number: 2015901710

LCCN Imprint Name: Suffolk, Virginia

Please visit our website at *www.PavingYourPath.com*

PAVING YOUR PATH PUBLISHING   Paving Your Path Publishing
445 N Main Street #206, Suffolk, VA 23439

Contents

List of Figures

Cover and book design: Phyllis McKee

Photo credits:
Jeff Lurie: Troy Shelton Photography
Capt. Danny Coyle: Mark Stockwell

This project was partially funded with the generous donations from:

Joseph Lurie

James Babor
Christina Gardner
Hunter Harville
Michael Harville
Todd Lyons
Sergey Solodyankin
Paul C. Venable, IV
Adam Wallick

Wendy Fennell
Lindsay Upton
Marcelo

An extra special thanks to Joseph Lurie, my brother, as a Power Donor! In addition to his financial support to this project, he played a key role in guiding me through adolescence to become the man that I am today.

Thank you, Joe!

*To the honor of those who don the Badge
and to their families...*

In Memory of
Captain Daniel "Danny" Coyle

I MET CAPTAIN DANNY COYLE during the early years of my life while he held the rank of sergeant. His personality and demeanor were unique and very special to me and to the residents of North Attleboro, MA. He was an inspiration to the community and a positive role model for thousands of youth throughout his career. He led me through some difficult times while I was growing up and continued as a support system for me through my high school years. Captain Coyle provided letters of recommendation for college and for my first position in law enforcement as a 9-1-1 dispatcher. As he rose through the ranks of lieutenant and captain, he continued his efforts in reaching out to community youth. You could always find Captain Coyle at local school sporting events or the annual Firefighters' Kids Day festivities. He was the definition of a true American hero in law enforcement.

Captain Coyle's positive influence on me has played a major role in my success as a law enforcement officer. In 2009, I met with him for coffee and told him that I was applying to a municipal police department in Virginia. A few days later, he called to tell me that he had written a letter of recommendation for me and that he was proud of my achievements. I was offered the position and started on July 1, 2009. Captain Coyle passed on July 9, 2009.

I will never forget everything that he so selflessly did to guide me in the right direction. I have dedicated this book, *Paving Your Path to Policing*, to his memory.

I will always remember you, Danny. Rest easy, brother.

Introduction

THE HISTORICAL EVOLUTION OF LAW ENFORCEMENT IN AMERICA has succumbed to the introduction of a new dramatic television series every season. The public perception of police officers has evolved from the doughnut-eating slob to the fashion-trendy detective, and most of the general public will never *really* understand what we do. The majority of a police officer's shift consists of paperwork and customer service. Every once in a while, a hot call comes in, followed by a brief rush of adrenaline. Take special note that the adrenaline rush is *brief* and then concludes with several hours of evidence inventory, report writing, case file preparation, and eventually court testimony. Yet every time you change the channel, you watch a SWAT team executing a high-risk search warrant, an action-packed car chase involving a fleeing felon, or an officer chasing down a suspect in a heated foot pursuit.

It is important to understand that not all crimes are solved in the sixty-minute block allotted by the network or in the forty-eight hours following the offense. Action-packed police shows are certainly entertaining, and to an extent, the procedures are accurate. However, real life does not afford police the opportunity to snap a photograph of a fingerprint with a cell phone and then immediately display the name, address, and next of kin of the victim. In some circumstances, these cop shows can actually make police work more difficult. Some agencies have experienced an increase in complaints when forensics personnel inform victims that there is no significant

evidence to collect in a particular case. The citizens argue that they have seen it on TV, so they know it can be done.

We see people in their worst states of peril. We see addiction. We see poverty. We see death, disease, and disaster. We rush toward gunfire while others run away. It is against our policies to display cowardice. We provide initial emergency medical care to victims of gunshot wounds, stabbings, sexual assaults, and vehicular crashes. We counsel our citizens through their most difficult moments.

The general public thrives on police stories. Human nature creates the desire to be where the action is. Do you remember the last time you were sitting in traffic for an hour on the interstate just to find out that there was a crash on the other side of the median? There is no true reason for traffic on the opposite side of the highway to be slowing to a near stop just so people can see how bad the crash is. This phenomenon has been commonly referred to as *blue light curiosity*. The natural instinct to watch police in action creates a certain awareness that officers are under constant scrutiny. Police officers are encouraged to operate at all times as if they are being monitored by audio and video recordings and that their actions may end up on the evening news or posted in online media outlets such as YouTube and Facebook.

A patrol supervisor commented during my squad's Roll Call one evening, "If you're where you're supposed to be, when you're supposed to be there, wearing the appropriate uniform, and doing what you're supposed to be doing, I will always have your back." Understand that we as police officers are representatives of government. We wear our badges as symbols of authority. It is our promise to abide by the laws we are sworn to uphold. Our mission is clear. However, our actions are almost always scrutinized. We remain under the careful watch of the public eye as we, Big Brother, continue to maintain law and order.

Police work is physically, mentally, and emotionally draining on a person. Not all people can deal with the pressure. Not all people can accept that you cannot save every person. Not all people can tell a parent that his or her teenage child was just involved in a vehicle crash and will not be coming home ever again. Being a police officer is not all about fast cars and action. Law enforcement is a serious profession. Now is the time to ask yourself whether you can handle it. If the answer is yes, this book will help you get there.

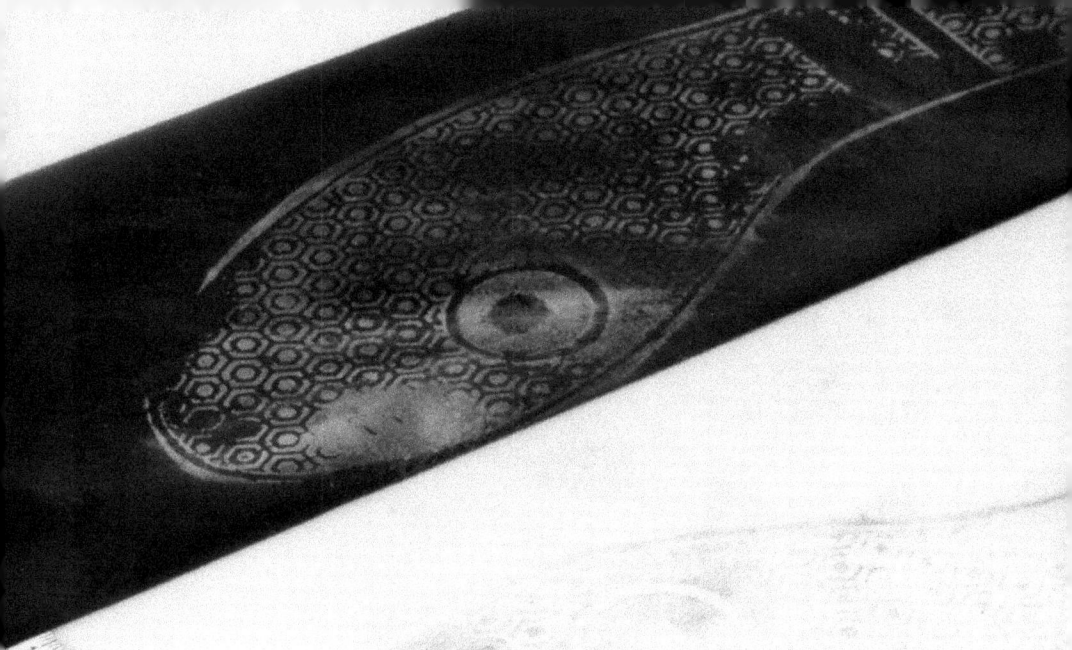

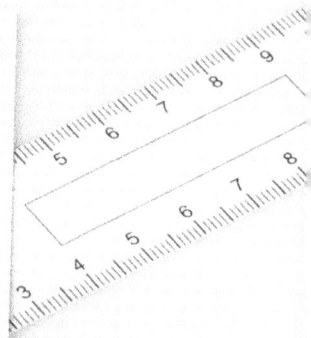

- Understanding career requirements

- Developing a Life Plan

- Choosing what kind of department
  to work for

- Choosing where to apply

CHAPTER 1

Developing an Action Plan

So you want to be a cop. Well, there are a few things I think you need to know before you start. Law enforcement as a profession is not all guts and glory. From filling out the initial application to the badge pinning ceremony, just getting to the streets takes nearly a year of hard work and dedication. As you embark on your journey, you will experience rotating shifts, inclement weather conditions, extended hours on weekends and holidays, and very little compensation to boot. Becoming a police officer is something you have to really want. It is something that requires support from your family and friends. It is an honorable profession through which your positive morals and values will be challenged every day by criticism and despair. If you are ready to stand among the largest brotherhood and sisterhood in the world, then I challenge you to become a police officer.

I have carefully designed this book to provide you with a guideline for appropriately constructing your résumé, networking with agency background investigators, enhancing your interview skills, and preparing for initial police academy training. The information contained within has been proven to enhance the marketability of any entry-level police officer candidate. Please be aware that most law enforcement agencies provide candidates with a list of automatic disqualifiers. If any of the agency's disqualifiers apply to you, then no book or preparation will change your ineligibility. However, if you meet the agency's minimum qualifications and you follow the simple lessons provided, you will be a strong step ahead of your competition.

Most agencies require the same basic qualifications. You must be twenty-one years of age at the time of appointment, possess a high school diploma or general equivalency degree (GED), and be able to successfully pass a criminal history and background check.

Some sheriff's offices will appoint deputy trainees at eighteen years of age, but there are restrictions in their initial duty assignments. Although these agencies list their minimum requirements, police officer candidates are seldom selected based solely upon the minimum. Law enforcement agencies receive a constant flow of résumés, which provides the administration with the utmost control during the selection process. Although federal laws provide certain protections under the Equal Opportunity Employment Act, the agencies will make every effort to appoint a balance of age, gender, and race.

America is a proud nation of growth and possibility. With the nearly unlimited diversity of our nation, it is imperative that you as the police officer candidate recognize the need to prove your worth to the agency you wish to work for. The ability to speak, to read, and to understand a second language will almost always enhance your opportunity for employment in any field. Depending on the agency, a multilingual candidate could be the deciding factor, even if it means stretching the budget to make it happen. One thing is for certain: law enforcement is a growing business. Regardless of recession, depression, or the peak of a prosperous economy, there will be a need for this invaluable service to the community.

> "Regardless of recession, depression, or the peak of a prosperous economy, there will be a need for this invaluable service to the community."

In future chapters, you will find that there are many different paths to policing. Together, we will examine the value of education, military experience, networking, physical fitness, and on-the-job training. The purpose is not to claim that one path is more appropriate than another, but to shed light on a variety of opportunities and the most efficient method to accomplishing your goal.

There are two major theories to be addressed: The first is to live life one day at a time. This theory sounds great and would suffice just fine if your goal were to obtain an entry-level position in a nine-to-five office. But when you are battling for a career in a highly competitive field, one day at a time just will not cut it. The second theory is to have a five-, ten-, or twenty-year plan. This book is designed to help you draw out that plan and to enhance your marketability in the law enforcement community. Now is the time for you to set yourself up for success. Now is the time to be one step ahead of the competition. Now is the time to pave *your* path to policing.

The first step to becoming a police officer is to choose a department that you would want to work for. All potential candidates have their own reasons as to why they want to become police officers.

But they don't always think about their careers as a whole. You certainly do not need to decide right now whether you want to be the chief some day, but you should have a general idea of what you would like to do within the department. For example, before I started submitting my applications, I knew that I wanted to work on a K9 unit. With that in mind, I had no reason to apply to a police department that did not have a K9 unit. (In some cases, I would recommend that you apply to every department that is hiring just to get your foot in the door, but that comes only after your choice departments have been exhausted. Most departments have a section on their applications where you must indicate the other police departments you have applied to. For that reason, the "apply to as many departments as I can" approach may cause more harm than good. You want to be able to tell your background investigator that that department is the one you want to work for. That message may be difficult to convey with a list of applications floating around.)

When you have a specialty unit or general career path in mind, make a list of at least ten departments who offer your desired option. Next, narrow your selection by determining your preference in the size of the department (number of sworn personnel), the population and classification of the jurisdiction (city, town, or county), and the compensation package offered for entry-level officers. Be sure to include your family members and close companions in this step as it could have a major impact on their ways of life as well.

You should now have a list of five to ten police departments that you would be interested in working for. Have you determined whether you will be living within the jurisdiction where you work? Have you discussed with your family members whether they are willing to relocate to a different city, county, or state? There are certainly pros and cons to both ends. Living outside of the jurisdiction will separate you and your family from running into people at the grocery store whom you have arrested or issued a traffic ticket to in the past. However, residing within the jurisdiction may entitle you to additional benefits, such as an assigned take-home police car. During this decision phase, it's important not only to research the police department, but to study other aspects of the jurisdiction, including the school system, hospitals, property tax rates, and available employment opportunities for your spouse or other family members. These types of statistics are available at the local city hall or office of tourism.

Hopefully, all of the departments you have chosen are currently hiring. If not, now is the time to narrow your list even further. If you have properly evaluated your selections, there should be three to five police departments remaining on your list. If you have not already done so, review the entire website for each department. The home page usually has a hyperlink to the recruitment or training section. This page is a great resource and should include whether the department is actively seeking qualified candidates, the appropriate contact information, and application deadlines. Most department websites will also include photographs, video clips, and brief descriptions of the specialized units offered. Be sure to note any personnel who are listed as the commander of a division (usually a captain, lieutenant, or sergeant) as these names will be important to have handy when reading Chapter 7, "Networking and Social Media." You don't need to memorize the names of every supervising official within the department, but putting a name to the face is helpful when it comes time for the panel interview. Often times, there will also be a "Message from the Chief" section on the department's website. Read it. And for heaven's sake, remember the chief's name!

> **"Most department websites will also include photographs, video clips, and brief descriptions of the specialized units offered."**

Congratulations. You have completed the first step to becoming a police officer. One of the greatest downfalls of a police officer candidate is failure to research the agency that you are applying to. In the next chapter, I provide you with direction for establishing initial contact with the department's recruitment or training coordinator. The first impression is a key factor in your success as a police officer candidate. In this step, you will be labeled. Your conduct and level of preparation will determine whether the label is positive or negative. If you follow the simple instructions provided, you will be presented as a squared-away professional who is ready to work hard to earn your place within the department.

It was May 19, 2012, a Saturday morning. I was in the parking lot at General Rental with my dad, who had traveled from out of town for the weekend to help me build a fence. As we loaded the posthole auger into the bed of his Ford pickup truck, I could hear the sirens in the distance. Thinking nothing of it, we continued to adjust the tie-down straps. Seconds later, an unmarked Crown Victoria with tinted windows sped past with lights flashing and sirens blazing. I remember touching my hand to my pants pocket in search of my phone. I asked my dad to reassure me, "It is Saturday, right?" He turned to me with a confused grin and responded, "Yeah, why?" I stood there for a moment, thinking. There couldn't be a parade today, because I would be working the overtime detail. But it was Saturday, and that was the precinct captain's car. He works Monday through Friday. And he never runs lights and sirens to a call. I turned back to my dad and said, "Something's wrong. We've gotta go."

Without hesitation, he knew it was serious, and we were on our way. We pulled up to the house, and I ran inside to check my phone. There were two missed calls from dispatch and one from the lieutenant. My partner in the detective bureau lived across the street at the time and was coming outside to see me. He had a blank look on his face, and my throat sank to the pit of my stomach. "Officer down!" he said. "We've gotta roll, bro."

I ran inside to grab my police car keys, gun, badge, and tactical vest. I gave my wife and son a kiss, and told them I'd be home soon. With lights and sirens, my partner and I were both on our way. I called dispatch to advise that we were en route to the scene. She advised that an officer had been involved in a foot pursuit after stopping a stolen vehicle. The officer was attacked in the woods, and the dispatchers lost radio contact. The first responding officers located the officer in the woods. He was

unconscious and brutally beaten. The advanced life support helicopter had responded and was presently transporting the officer to the region's level-one trauma center for emergency surgery. At the time, it was unclear whether the officer would live.

As we arrived to the scene, there were police vehicles as far as I could see. A perimeter had been established; it was believed that the offender was somewhere within the approximately two-mile area. There were SWAT officers, K9 teams, uniform patrol officers, detectives, firefighters, and even state police motorcycle officers who had shown up, without request, to help out in any way that they could. A police helicopter was circling the airspace above. Our agency did not even have a helicopter, so I wasn't sure where it had come from at the time. Police agencies from across the region sent manpower to assist with the soon-to-be all-day manhunt for the offender, a previously convicted violent felon.

Reaction teams made every effort to use alternate radio channels since the offender had stolen the officer's portable radio from his duty belt. Additional units were staged in adjoining cities, ready to deploy if it was determined that the offender had made it outside of the perimeter. The area search was nearly completed when SWAT members spotted the offender at the woods line. Facing the business-end of a half dozen M4 assault rifles, the offender raised his empty hands and surrendered in front of the news media approximately nine hours after the operation began.

The entire community came together to support the officer and his family. There were bake sales, car washes, and other fundraisers to provide monetary support for the household during his hospitalization. After numerous reconstructive surgeries and physical therapy, the officer was able to return home to his family. Out of respect for the officer's privacy, I won't disclose his identity or current status.

As for the offender, he pleaded guilty to several felony offenses and was issued the maximum possible sentence by a Virginia Circuit Court Judge: life plus forty years in prison.

- Strategy of the initial contact

- Saying "Thank you" can be
  used to your advantage

- Making a great first impression

CHAPTER 2

Initial Contact: When You Have Only One Shot, Make It Count

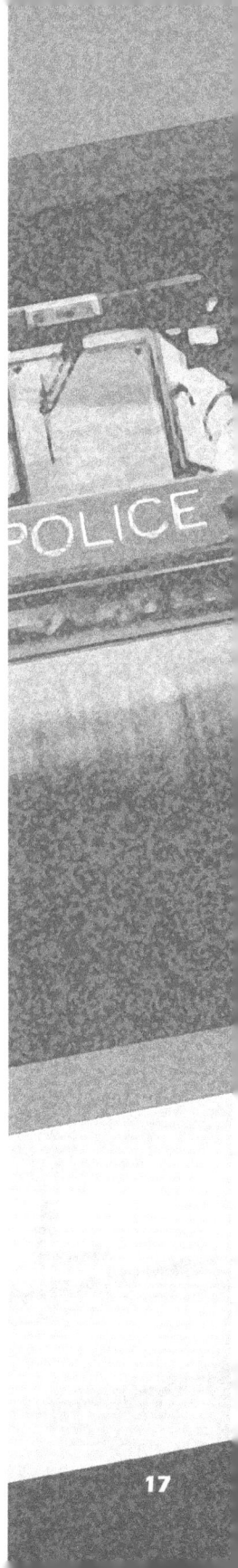

You have carefully selected three to five police departments to which you will apply as a police officer candidate. The next step is to contact the Office of Professional Standards, human resources, or recruiting unit. You can usually find the appropriate contact information for most police departments online. There are, however, hundreds of small town and small county departments throughout the country (usually consisting of fewer than thirty members) who lack the manpower to establish such specialized divisions. In this case, there is usually a ranking official, sergeant or higher, who has been designated as the training coordinator.

If the required contact information doesn't appear on the agency's website, contact the police communications center via the published business line during normal business hours to request the information. The dispatcher will most likely ask if you would like to be connected to the appropriate official or to that person's voice mail. Although it is not necessary at this time, you may choose to speak with the person briefly. Prior to being transferred, ask the dispatcher for the official's rank, correct spelling of his or her name, and direct telephone number for future use.

Some people are more confident speaking in person than they are on the telephone. If this is the case with you, simply advise the dispatcher that you do not need to speak with the official right now, but would like the appropriate contact information for future correspondence. The dispatcher should then provide you with the official's rank, name, e-mail address, and office telephone number.

"Remember that a first impression is very important."

Remember that a first impression is very important. Simply introduce yourself, advise the official that you wish to apply as a police officer candidate, and ask if you may e-mail him or her your résumé and cover letter for review. The official may tell you not to e-mail, but to instead fill out an application and drop it off at police headquarters or human resources.

Do not e-mail an official who tells you not to. It is important to recognize that this is the person who will determine whether you are worthy of continuing in the hiring process. Listen to what the official says and carefully follow those instructions.

In most cases, the official will be happy to accept your information for review. At this point, be sure to verify the correct spelling of the official's name, as well as his or her rank and department e-mail address. Always thank the person for taking the time to speak with you and reinforce that you look forward to speaking again soon. When you thank the official, use the person's rank and last name. This approach not only shows the official that you are respectful and were paying attention, but also inadvertently helps you remember the correct pronunciation of their name. For example, say, "Thank you, Lieutenant Baldwin. I appreciate your help. I look forward to speaking with you soon."

If the official is unavailable and you are transferred to voice mail, you must be prepared to leave a message. The content of a voice message is just as important as, if not more important than, actually speaking with the official. The logic is that the voice message can be saved and replayed for review. You certainly do not want to sound like you are reading from a script, but it may be helpful to write down what you plan to say prior to making the call. Speak clearly and enunciate your words. Refrain from using "umm" and "ah" during pauses. Be certain to state your first and last name, contact telephone number, and e-mail address. If your name may be hard to understand, it is acceptable to spell it during the voice message. Again, your closing remarks are vital and should be as if you are speaking directly with the official. For example, "Thank you, Lieutenant Baldwin. I look forward to speaking with you soon."

"…it is always a good practice to send a follow-up letter"

If you do speak with the appropriate official, it is always a good practice to send a follow-up letter within a few days of the conversation. Often, an applicant makes the mistake of combining the follow-up letter with the cover letter. Some would argue that the combination allows the cover letter to become more personalized toward the recruiter. But what happens when that letter travels up the chain with your résumé to the human resources specialist, city government officials, or the chief of police? A letter should only be personalized to the intended recipient when it is not meant to be forwarded beyond that recipient. If the letter caters specifically to the recruiter, then it becomes meaningless to other personnel.

The purpose of the follow-up letter is twofold: to thank an official for taking time to speak with you and to put your name in front of that person as often as possible. A recruiter speaks with dozens of applicants on a daily basis. Your objective is to stand out among them all. You want the person to remember you as the process moves along, and sending separate follow-up and cover letters helps achieve that goal. Why would you combine the two letters and have the official see your name only once when he or she can see it twice, right?

The major difference between the cover letter and the follow-up letter is that the follow-up letter is not all about you. The follow-up letter is to show the official not only that you were paying attention to what he or she told you, but also that you appreciate his or her assistance and you look forward to working together. **Figure 1** is an example of a follow-up letter utilized after speaking with the recruiting official via telephone.

If you had the opportunity to speak with the official and he or she recommended meeting in person, or if you were able to schedule an appointment to speak with him or her further, then you should take some time to prepare specific questions well before the day of the meeting. Keep your inquiries brief and to the point. Things that you may wish to ask may be associated with the hiring process, the academy, or how to set up a ride-along. If you have not invested in professional business attire, now is the time to make it happen. Whether you're attending a meeting or simply dropping off some paperwork, every impression counts. Business attire for males is a dress suit and tie or dress slacks and a sport coat; for females, it is a dress suit or dress slacks and a blouse with, at minimum, quarter-length sleeves.

Walking into the official's office for the first time may seem intimidating. A good trick is to relate to the official on a non-law enforcement level if possible. For example, if you see a ballpark photograph on the office wall and you are a fan of the same team, use that shared interest to your advantage. If you were a United States Marine and you notice the eagle, globe, and anchor paperweight on the official's desk, break the ice by indicating that you were a Marine and asking about the official's service. But keep it short and sweet. Understanding that the official's position is to learn as much as he or she can about each police officer candidate, your objective should be to get your point across by saying as little as possible.

Figure 1 Initial Phone Call Follow-up Letter

January 17, 2015

Your N. Here
123 Main Street, Apt B
Anytown, MA 12345

Lieutenant David Baldwin
Anywhere Police Department
456 Washington Street
Anywhere, VA 67890

Dear Lieutenant Baldwin,

It was a pleasure speaking with you this afternoon. Thank you for describing the many different specialized units that the department operates. Our conversation positively reinforced my desire to earn a position as an Anywhere Police Officer. I appreciate that you took so much time to explain the details of the hiring process to me.

I understand that the hiring process is competitive and would like to take this opportunity to thank you in advance for your time and consideration. I look forward to hearing from you.

Respectfully,

Your Signature

Your N. Here
(508) 555.1234
Youraddress@domain.com

Figures **2** and **3** are examples of standard follow-up letters after meeting in person with the department official.

Take note of the paragraph format in the sample follow-up letters. This should be the format of any professional correspondence you write. The addresses, greeting, body, and salutation should all line up on the left margin. The date should be the only item that lines up to the right margin. The body of the letter should line up to both margins evenly using the "justified" paragraph format. The closing signature should contain your name, phone number, and e-mail address. Always skip two lines between the salutation and your name at the end of the letter. This will allow ample space for you to sign the letter upon printing it. *Do not send a formal letter without signing it.* You should send a follow-up letter via regular US mail, not e-mail (unless the official specifically requires all contact by e-mail). If you are e-mailing any professional correspondence (follow-up letter, cover letter, etc) that would require a signature if sent by US mail, you should print the correspondence, sign it, scan it as a PDF or similar file (so that it cannot be edited), and send it as an attachment in the e-mail.

> **"**...it is vital that you follow instructions exactly as they are issued.**"**

As with any paramilitary organization, it is vital that you follow instructions exactly as they are issued. Be sure to ask for the official's preferred method of contact. If the official tells you that all correspondence should be e-mailed, then do not call. If the official tells you that all correspondence should be via telephone, then do not just show up at headquarters. There is a fine line between being a go-getter and being an annoyance. Make sure you play by the rules, and you will already be one giant step ahead of the other candidates. Most agencies receive between twenty and one hundred inquiries for employment on a monthly basis. Most recruiting officials will separate the application packages into two piles upon receipt. The professional-looking, well-put-together pile and the "I guess I'll keep it on file" pile. The latter usually never gets a second look. A good recruiter recognizes that the majority of police work is paperwork and report writing. If a police officer candidate cannot get the application package right, how can that person be expected to turn in an error-free report?

Figure 2 Standard Follow-up Letter 1

January 17, 2015

Your N. Here
123 Main Street, Apt B
Anytown, MA 12345

Lieutenant David Baldwin
Anywhere Police Department
456 Washington Street
Anywhere, VA 67890

Dear Lieutenant Baldwin,

It was a pleasure speaking with you at Anywhere Police Headquarters this afternoon. I am especially intrigued with the number of specialized units the department operates. I appreciate that you took so much time to explain the details of the hiring process to me. It is also good to know that the Anywhere Police Department employs such dedicated Red Sox fans. The photograph on your wall of you and your son on the pitcher's mound at Fenway Park was impressive.

I understand that the hiring process is competitive and would like to take this opportunity to thank you in advance for your time and consideration. I look forward to hearing from you.

Respectfully,

Your Signature

Your N. Here
(508) 555.1234
Youraddress@domain.com

Figure 3 Standard Follow-up Letter 2

January 17, 2015

Your N. Here
123 Main Street Apt B
Anytown, MA 12345

Lieutenant David Baldwin
Anywhere Police Department
456 Washington Street
Anywhere, VA 67890

Dear Lieutenant Baldwin,

It was a pleasure speaking with you at Anywhere Police Headquarters this afternoon. I am especially intrigued with the number of specialized units the department operates. I appreciate that you took so much time to explain the details of the hiring process to me. Thank you for sharing your military-to-civilian life transitional tips with me, too. Everything you said makes perfect sense, and that is exactly where I am in life right now.

I understand that the hiring process is competitive and would like to take this opportunity to thank you in advance for your time and consideration. I look forward to hearing from you.

Respectfully,

Your Signature

Your N. Here
(508) 555.1234
Youraddress@domain.com

It was July 4th. The day began as just another holiday. I brewed a morning cup of coffee and prepared for a day with the family. We piled into the car, traveled to the grocery store for a few last-minute items, and quickly returned home to fire up the grill. The afternoon consisted of hamburgers, hotdogs, bratwurst, and the company of family and friends. The afternoon faded into the early evening, and it was almost time to go to work. I was assigned to work a police detail at the local Independence Day fireworks event. As I prepared for my shift, my boots were polished, my shirt was pressed, and my pants were creased. I wrapped my duty belt around my waist, turned my portable radio on, and went to the living room to give my wife and son a kiss. I told them that I loved them, and then I walked out the door toward my marked police car at the roadside.

As soon as I put my key into the driver side door, I heard the sound that makes every officer cringe: The priority-one tone came across the air. I turned the volume up slightly and listened attentively. The dispatcher announced, "Unconscious person, priority one. Unconscious person, priority one. Any unit that can respond. Eleven-month-old male, unresponsive and not breathing." At the time, my son was only eleven months old. It immediately hit home. As I jumped into my police car, the dispatcher announced the name of the street. I remember thinking, "Wait a second. That's my neighborhood."

I was the first officer on the scene. As I approached, the panic-stricken mother and father stood by frantically in their front yard. The father was holding their child. He ran to me. There was blood around the child's nose and mouth. As I assessed the child, I donned my protective gloves and confirmed for dispatch that he was unconscious and not alert. I requested additional units and for EMS to step it up. I looked inside the child's mouth and noticed there was an obstruction. I performed a finger sweep, but the object would not dislodge. I turned the child facedown over my left forearm and performed several back blows. Upon turning him back over, I performed a second finger sweep. I removed a piece of food from the child's airway, and he swallowed the other piece. The child began to cry and scream. As the paramedics and additional units arrived, I relinquished the child to medical personnel and turned to console the parents. Other officers quickly took over for me so that I could take in what had just occurred. One of the paramedics shook my hand and said, "Good job. Looks like he's gonna make it. You saved that kid's life." It seemed like nothing to me at the time.

Once I made sure the other officers had everything covered, I told them I had to report to the fireworks detail, and I was on my way. It was not until I was in my police car by myself that reality set in. **Wow. That was crazy. I didn't even think. It happened just like they taught us.**

Remember, the more that you train, the luckier you appear. I saved a life that day. If I do nothing more with my career, I know that I've made a difference. Are you ready?

- Market yourself properly with a position-specific résumé

- Making the most of your relevant education and experience

CHAPTER 3

Under Construction: The Road to Your Résumé

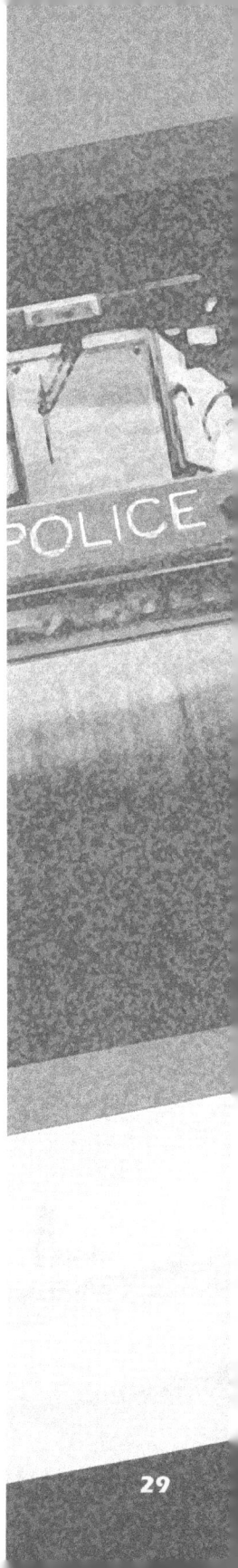

ONCE YOU HAVE ESTABLISHED a point of contact, whether you spoke with the official or left a voice message, it is time to customize your résumé and cover letter for presentation. Bear in mind that there are quite a few people involved with the hiring process to whom you have not yet been introduced. Your résumé is their first impression, so it should convey all necessary information pertaining to your ability to perform the desired position. Put yourself in their shoes and understand that, at this point, they can only determine who you are by reading about you. You will have the opportunity to elaborate on your qualifications throughout the interview process. But for now, let us focus on what I call the "impact points."

We will begin by establishing the basic rules of résumé writing. One of the most important impact points is to keep the length of your résumé to one page, if possible. For an entry-level position, that should not be a problem. As with your cover letter, the résumé is designed to provide important information in a quick, simple manner. Your résumé should begin with a heading and should contain your objective, educational achievements, work experience pertaining to your desired career path, and miscellaneous awards or certifications as applicable. Do not be discouraged if your résumé is on the bare side. One great advantage to maintaining an updated résumé is that you will see yourself developing professionally each time you add something to the education or achievements sections. Always save previous copies of your résumé for your records. There will come a time when you have so much training and so many certifications that you will be removing less significant items from the page. The copies of your previous résumés will come in handy when it is time to go back and remember those dates. It is also somewhat of a reward in itself when you look back five years from now at your original résumé to see how far you have come.

The first thing that your potential employer sees is the heading of your résumé. There will be a point in the hiring process where the background investigators will be flipping through the pages of your application package. You need your résumé to jump out at them. There is a fine line between plain and extravagant. **Figure 4** below is an example of your basic résumé heading. Note that the name line is in bold print and is slightly larger than the rest of the heading. Be sure to list the phone number that you are most likely to be reached at. There are plenty of employers out there who, if they call and reach your voice mail, will hang up and move on to the next candidate. Your heading should be centered at the top of the page, aligned with the one-inch top margin.

Figure 4 Resume Heading

Your N. Here
123 Main Street Apt B
Anytown, MA 12345
(508) 555.1234
Youraddress@domain.com

The contact information that you choose to provide should be uniform throughout all future correspondence. If you don't already have professional-looking e-mail address, now is a good time to create a new e-mail account. For example, if your e-mail address is something like *SlamDunkKing@whatever.net* or *LadiesMan123@whatever.net*, it's got to go. For a professional appearance, try several different domains like Gmail, Yahoo Mail, or any of the other free services to obtain an account using only your first and last name. For example, if your name is John Doe and e-mail address *JohnDoe@gmail.com* is unavailable, try *JohnDoe@yahoo.com* or *JohnDoe1@yourchoiceofdomain.com*. By providing a more identifiable e-mail address with your résumé, the employer will begin to see your name more and more. Depending on the amount of free space in your résumé, you may choose to add a basic separation line underneath your heading just before your objective. Not only will the line add to the professional appearance of your résumé, but it can also fill in empty space until you have enough training and experience to fill the page.

> "By providing a more identifiable e-mail address with your résumé, the employer will begin to see your name more and more."

The objective should be aligned just below the heading and to the edge of the one-inch left margin. Separate the heading and the objective either by skipping one line or by using the separation line as described above. The heading "Objective" should be in bold print to stand out because it is the section title. The objective is your opportunity to be very clear with the recruiter. Often, candidates are way too vague in describing their goals, or they simply do not list an objective at all. The purpose of listing your objective is to provide the recruiter with a general idea of your personal goal within the agency. **Figure 5** is an example of a weak objective.

Figure 5 Example of a Weak Objective

Objective: To become a police officer and to make a difference in my community.

This objective sounds nice, but is it really your career objective to just become a police officer and never advance or transfer to a specialized unit? If so, that is perfectly acceptable. However, there is a huge difference between getting a job and earning a career. Becoming a police officer is something that must be earned. If you plan to move from uniform patrol to the detectives or a narcotics unit, or to earn a supervisory position advancing to sergeant and higher, then now is the time to project those goals in a well-rounded, all-inclusive statement. Now is the time to tell your recruiter, "I'm not looking to get my feet wet and then leave; I plan to make something of myself and be with this department until I retire." Take some time to put a little more thought into your objective. **Figure 6** is an example of a strong objective.

Figure 6 Example of a Strong Objective

Objective: To earn a progressive position within the Anywhere Police Department where strong written and verbal communication skills are necessary.

Let's break it down. There are a few important points within this objective. First and foremost, you are telling the recruiter that you understand this is a competitive process and are willing and ready to work hard to earn the position. Secondly, mentioning "a progressive position" indicates that you are not seeking an entry-level position only; you will continue to train and educate yourself within your field so that internal advancement becomes an option. You specify the name of the department you are applying to so that the statement is clear: Out of all the police departments that are actively recruiting, you want to work for the Anywhere Police Department. Of course, if you are applying to multiple agencies, make sure you change the objective to list the name of the agency that you are applying to for each application! Lastly, as you learned in previous chapters, the majority of police work is paperwork and customer service. You are acknowledging that you understand the importance and appropriate use of verbal and nonverbal communication skills by including "where strong written and verbal communication skills are necessary." There is a lot going on within this short sentence, but the objective should be an "in your face" statement to the recruiter explaining exactly what you intend to accomplish if hired. The objective alone could be the deciding factor in hiring you over another candidate.

Immediately following the objective will be your educational achievements. As with the objective, the title "Education" should be bolded and aligned just below the previous title and to the edge of the one-inch left margin. Your educational achievements should be listed in reverse chronological order (beginning with the most recent). Each entry should include the name of the educational institution, the city and state of the campus, the dates attended, and the relevant credentials earned. See **Figures** 7 and **8** as examples below.

Figure 7 Education, Example 1

Education:	Anywhere University, Anytown, MA
	Bachelor of Arts in Criminal Justice—May 2011
	Magna Cum Laude 3.80 GPA
	Small Town High School, Small Town, FL
	High-School Diploma—June 2007

Figure 8 Education, Example 2

Education:	United States Coast Guard Academy, New London, CT
	Bachelor of Science in Homeland Defense—May 2011
	Certificate in Maritime Security Studies—May 2011
	Big Blue Regional Vocational School, Somewhere, GA
	High School Diploma—June 2007

In **Figure 7**, the student had achieved an outstanding grade-point average, which is indicated in italic print just below the relevant credential. If you achieved a grade-point average of 3.60 or above on a 4.00 scale, you may include it in this section. You shouldn't include anything below a 3.60 grade-point average. In **Figure 8**, the student attended a military academy and earned an undergraduate certificate in addition to the bachelor's degree. You should include any formal classroom or online education in the education section. If you enlisted in the military or entered the workforce immediately following high school graduation, the high school information will be the only education listed. The exception to this rule is if you have completed an accredited law enforcement or corrections academy or an officially recognized military specialty school (flight school, special forces, officer candidate school, etc.). This situation may occur if you are transitioning from the military or employment in the city or county jail to becoming a police officer. See **Figure 9** below.

Figure 9 Including Accredited Military or Law Enforcement Education

Education: Smallville Criminal Justice Training Academy, Smallville, NY
Basic Corrections Officer Course—May 2009

Lake Taylor High School, Lake Taylor, MD
High School Diploma—June 2007

The next section in your résumé, referred to as "Course Highlights," is optional. You may use it to fill space until you earn enough law enforcement-related certifications to complete the page. The title "Course Highlights" should be aligned just below the previous title and to the edge of the one-inch left margin. Your course highlights will consist of anything that you feel is appropriate to list. Primarily, these should be college-level courses, but there are a few exceptions. Nowadays, many high schools, in particular those with a vocational option, may offer a forensics or cyber security elective to students with an interest in law enforcement. You may list these courses, along with any public speaking or government-related courses, as shown below in **Figure 10**. Also note any foreign languages that you may have studied and are proficient in (this is especially important if you aspire to work in a culturally diverse area).

Figure 10 Showing Related Course Highlights

Course Highlights: Introduction to Forensics; American Government; Public Speaking Seminar; Spanish I, II, and III.

I encourage every person, regardless of your career path, to make every effort to learn a foreign language. In most recent studies conducted by various colleges and census organizations, the cultural base of the United States has become increasingly diverse. A multilingual police officer candidate will, without a doubt, have an advantage over a candidate who only speaks English.

Following the "Course Highlights" section will be your "Experience" section. As you progress within your career, this section will contain only law enforcement-related employment. However, for the time being, a recruiter is looking for indicators of dedication and initiative. Any customer service or leadership positions are especially desirable. Note that this section is titled "Experience" because you may list internships or volunteer activities, too. If your only work experience is your high school job at McDonald's, but you advanced from cashier to shift leader during your tenure there, then the experience is relevant. There are methods of providing accurate and honest information in describing your employment while articulating the importance of your position. For example, you were a cashier, but that was not your only function. You were the greeter, cashier, and first line of customer care, right? So spotlight it! Your experience would be documented in a similar manner as the previous sections. See **Figure 11** below.

Figure 11 Taking Credit for Relevant Experience

Experience: Guest Services Representative, McDonald's #1478
Front Line Supervisor, promotion issued July 2007
Small Town, NY May 2006 –

In **Figure 11**, you are providing a more professional title than Cashier by encompassing all of your tasks into the description of "Guest Services Representative." Remember, the interview process will afford you the opportunity to elaborate on any specific tasks performed. Note that the second line indicates the promotion to a leadership position and the date of promotion. This section is very important to show your recruiter not only that you have the ability to work well with others but also that your previous supervisor has entrusted you with the responsibility to supervise others.

Any volunteer experience (such as working with Habitat for Humanity, helping local food banks or shelters, or participating in a neighborhood crime watch or National Night Out) would also be listed in the "Experience" section. If you want to include any additional skills or certifications, you may create a final section titled "Additional Skills and Training." One very easy way to build your résumé is to enroll in free training courses. The Department of Homeland Security and the Federal Emergency Management Administration offer free online courses through the *www.fema.gov* web page. (You will have to create an account on the web page under the "Independent Study" section.) These simple online courses will provide a great knowledge base regarding the National Incident Management System and the basics of emergency preparedness. In fact, most police departments require these courses as part of your initial field training. I had completed the online courses prior to my employment and was able to submit the certificates of completion to the recruiter. I was then exempt from the additional training requirement!

> **"One very easy way to build your résumé is to enroll in free training courses."**

When applying for an entry-level position in any career field, the main objective is to shine above all others in a positive manner. For a little extra spark, purchase résumé paper from your local office supply store. Résumé paper is a slightly heavier weight and has more visual texture than traditional copy paper. Print only your cover letter and résumé on the special paper. All other documentation included in your application package should be on plain white copy paper. That way, your cover letter and résumé will stand out, and you can photocopy your other documentation without the paper's texture distorting the image. For presentation purposes, purchase a one-inch or half-inch three-ring binder with a clear insert sleeve on the front cover. Inside the binder, place your cover letter first, your résumé second, and all other supporting documentation in order of importance thereafter. Usually the documentation should be in the same order as the items appear on your résumé (diplomas and degrees, then training certificates, and finally miscellaneous awards). If you have letters of reference from prominent officials (police chief, sheriff, political figures, etc.), place them at the back of the package. Using résumé paper, create a standard cover page to put in the front clear insert sleeve. Near the center of the page, type your full name with middle initial. Toward the bottom of the page, type, "This portfolio has been specifically prepared as an application for" and then add the name of the agency you are applying to. *Do not add graphics to the cover page.*

Now the hard part is done. You are able to showcase yourself to the department in a professional and standardized manner. Your résumé should tell the brief outline of who you are. The interview and background process is designed to extract the details behind the résumé and is where you will have the opportunity to elaborate on your qualifications.

IN PREVIOUS DECADES, one of the most common places for a small town to locate its police department was in conjunction with other municipal buildings, such as the town hall. My first position in law enforcement was as an E9-1-1 and police dispatcher in Foxboro, Massachusetts. I began on the evening shift from 4:00 pm to midnight and was moved soon after to the permanent midnight shift. It was an enjoyable position. As the nighttime hours slowed down, I was able to complete some of my homework for courses that I was taking at a local community college. Foxboro had not developed to the magnitude that it is today. Gillette Stadium was not even a thought, never mind the enormity of the Patriot Place compound today.

The small town employed about thirty police officers. I was responsible for receiving 9-1-1 and police-service calls. There was a separate dispatcher over at the firehouse to whom I would transfer the fire-service calls. The officers would stop by to chat every now and again, but for the most part, it was just me in the building for more than half of the eight-hour shift. The police department was located in the basement of the town hall, and there was a set of stairs to lead citizens from the ground level down to the police department's lobby. The sole dispatcher was also responsible to serve as a customer-service representative for walk-ins.

One night stands out among any other that tested my abilities to the fullest. I was fighting with the computer system, as it would always freeze up during heavy storms. The thunder rattled the windows as the lightning cracked through the sky, lighting up the top edges of the windows with every strike. The old-style radio and communications systems were housed in a long, two-console, metal desk. The radio had burnt out a few months back, and the town's radio guy had wired an old police-vehicle radio to the panel. Picture this big black box with crimps and wires hanging out of the back and an old-school, coiled radio mic resting across the desk. Now picture a nondigital telephone system with a switchboard panel where you had to select each line before receiving or transferring calls. A dot-matrix printer in the corner would screech a deafening cry for a new ink tape at least twice per shift when the nightly state police administrative messages scrolled through. Yeah, that was my office.

As the morning hours approached, the storm grew stronger and stronger. I was holding the phone in my left hand talking to a citizen and holding the radio in my right hand about to dispatch a call for service when **bang!** I opened my eyes, and I was lying on the floor. The room was filled with smoke. A detective was standing over me with his gun drawn toward the front door. He was looking around in awe as if someone were there. "Jeff, Jeff, are you OK? What the hell happened?" There was a ringing in my ear, and I could hear some type of alarm off in the distance. It took me a second to realize what had happened. Some kind of explosion had knocked me right out of my chair. The computer screens were black, the thick metal desk twisted like a sheet of aluminum, the radio was blown, and the smell of smoke and burnt wiring filled the room. An alarm from the 9-1-1 backup console was beeping from the far end of the hallway. The detective said that he thought I had been shot when he heard it from the other room.

We quickly gained our composure and realized that lightning must have struck the building. The whole dispatch center was toast. There were no communications in or out for the officers or the citizens. Hurriedly, I grabbed my cell phone and called our secondary PSAP (public safety answering point). Every 9-1-1 center has a backup center to ensure there is always a 9-1-1 operator to answer the call. In this case, I contacted the Mansfield Police Department (the next town over), and all police and fire communications were transferred within minutes. Thankfully, no one was seriously injured. We later discovered that the lightning rod had been severed at the ground near the back of the building, which explained why none of the equipment was grounded. We presumed that the lightning rod must have been damaged when plow trucks pushed the snow against the building during the prior winter. Of course, there is no way of knowing how it happened.

Had I not been holding the phone and radio at the same time, it could have been the end. Did the electricity ground through me to the other equipment? Who knows? I received a commendation from the town manager and chief of police for quick action under pressure, and I have the newspaper article for my files. Other than that, it was just another day on the job. You never know what you'll encounter in this career.

- Tackling the written exam

- Recognizing the variation in testing procedures nationwide

CHAPTER 4
A Solid
Foundation

THE NUTS AND BOLTS of the police officer hiring process begins with a written examination and a physical abilities test. In the past, the written exam came first, followed by the interview and finally the physical abilities test. More recently, agencies are administering the written exam and the physical abilities test first. This way, they do not waste time interviewing candidates who lack the aptitude or the physical stamina to perform as a police officer.

The written exam can be presented in many variations. However, the content is often very similar. Most of the written exams are presented in a multiple-choice format specifically to accommodate computerized grading, which is more accurate. The computerized grading requires the candidate to fill in a standard answer form with a number-two pencil. The answer forms are then scanned through a computer grading device. Depending on the agency, you may be permitted to receive your score before departing the testing facility. Other agencies will mail you your scores within a week or so.

You should regard every step of the hiring process as part of your interview. That includes not just your personal appearance but also that of your vehicle. For example, on the morning of the Rhode Island State Police exam, State Troopers visually inspect recruit candidates' vehicles for equipment violations as the recruit candidates enter the parking lot. Recruit candidates are expected to move with urgency toward the staging area, where they are instructed to stand at attention in formation among other recruit candidates. State Troopers walk back and forth, inspecting the candidates for proper attire, proper grooming (hair and face), and appropriate posture. They also ensure that the recruit candidates possess the items required by the testing notice and that they do not possess any other items. If a recruit candidate does not possess the required items, is not dressed appropriately, or is not properly groomed, then that person is dismissed. The Rhode Island State Police, along with many other highly recognized and decorated agencies, is known for its paramilitary style and its demand for squared-away recruit candidates. The retention of personnel within such agencies is a direct reflection of their dedication and professionalism in law enforcement.

In other cases, like the Florida Department of Law Enforcement (FDLE) and many small- to medium-sized municipal agencies, testing is conducted as a basic standardized test given in a classroom environment by a non-law enforcement exam proctor. Although the requirements may be somewhat lax compared to paramilitary agencies, the recruit candidate's appearance and behavior remains a direct reflection on his or her character and professionalism. At least one member of an oral interview panel is often present, in or out of uniform, and is assigned to take notes, both positive and negative, about specific recruit candidates.

> "You should regard every step of the hiring process as part of your interview."

Your haircut and grooming are only part of the physical picture. It is imperative that all candidates wear appropriate professional courtroom attire. For males, appropriate courtroom attire is a dress suit and tie or dress slacks and a sport coat; for females, it is a dress suit or dress slacks and a blouse with, at minimum, quarter-length sleeves.

There are many variations of the written exam. Private companies all over the country are constantly proposing new testing styles to law enforcement administrations. Common testing procedures include observation and recall of video-based scenarios, critical analysis of written scenarios, and memorization and identification of printed photographs. The following are examples of each common testing procedure.

A video-based scenario may include observing a surveillance video from a convenience store armed robbery in progress. You are given an opportunity to observe the video and to take handwritten notes. Once completed, the video is not replayed. You are then tested on the ability to store and recall the incident. In this example, you may be asked to identify the name of the store being robbed, the color of the gunman's T-shirt, or in which hand the gun was held when pointed at the clerk.

Critical analysis of written scenarios may involve receiving a passage from an officer's incident report that may contain spelling and grammatical errors. You are then required to select the appropriate corrections from a multiple-choice list.

Lastly, the memorization and identification of printed photographs portion is often a point of difficulty. You are presented with mug shots of several individuals, as well as a brief synopsis of the incident that the person was suspected of. You view the photographs in a "Roll Call" environment and are permitted to take handwritten notes. Once all photographs have been shown, the memorization and identification portion of the written test begins. You are tasked with matching each photo to the name of the person by the description previously provided. The test ensures you have the basic memorization and observation skills required to effectively perform as a law enforcement officer.

As there are literally thousands of law enforcement agencies throughout the country, there is no way to accurately predict the testing methods employed by every agency. The written exam may be given on the same day as the physical agility test, before or after the physical test. It may be given on a separate day before or after the physical agility test. Regardless of the chronological placement of the written exam, it is important to eat nutritious meals during the day prior to the exam and to be well rested on the morning of the exam. By following the guidelines within this chapter, you will have a better understanding of the expectations and required preparation for the written exam. For some agencies, a study guide with sample questions is available, or the recruiting official may provide some insight as to what you should expect. It may sound silly, but you can practice memorization and strategic response simply by watching television with friends or family. For example, while watching any random television show, tell another person to write down a few questions during a five-minute time block. After the time has passed, have the person ask you the questions and see how you perform. If it is available, use DVR technology to rewind and confirm your answers. A little bit of practice goes a long way to sharpen your observation and memorization skills.

By now, you should have already implemented a structured aerobic and anerobic workout program into your daily routine. Generally, there are runners and there are weight lifters. To stand out among the best of the best, you need to be both. Focus on the core concepts of many physical agility tests. They often include running, sprinting, push-ups, sit-ups, and pull ups. More recently, agencies have incorporated an obstacle course to simulate job-related tasks, such as pursuit of a fleeing suspect. As always, you should consult your physician before beginning a new workout regiment.

AS THE EARLY MORNING HOURS APPROACHED, all I could think of was how close it was getting to 7:00 a.m. I was the midnight shift sergeant and, for anyone who has worked an overnight shift, the hours around 4:30 a.m. begin to really take a toll on you. If there is one thing that attracts the majority of people to law enforcement, it's that you never know what will happen next. I was headed back toward the precinct to complete some administrative tasks when everything changed. The priority-one tone cut through the deafening silence like a hot knife through butter as it came across the radio. "Dispatch to all units. Breaking and entering in progress. Shots fired. One victim with possible gunshot wound. Any unit that can respond."

As units responded, I recalled my experience as a detective, where I was assigned just a few months prior. I arrived on the scene, and my officers had set up a perimeter around the residence. A body lay motionless in the front doorway. As I approached, I realized that the victim was still alive. There was no time to think. There was no time to look around and ask who was in charge. It was me. I was in charge. And I needed to start making some quick decisions. Was the shooter still in the house? How many offenders were there? Were there other victims? How many officers do I have on the scene, and how many more do I need?

I posted behind cover near the front door with my handgun drawn and fixed on the entryway. I had police officers on the perimeter, and paramedics were on the way. The dispatcher came across the radio to ask me if the scene was secure for paramedics to respond. Usually, the paramedics would stage close by until police secure the scene and deem it safe for them to respond. In this case, there was no time. I responded to dispatch that the scene was not secure, but that police on scene would provide armed cover to the paramedics while they extricated the victim. I stood focused on the entryway with no backup behind me. I kept yelling, "Need one! Need one!" Suddenly, I felt a hand on my shoulder.

"I'm with you, Sarge." It was a senior officer with prior Army service. "Whatever you need, I'm with you," he said. Another officer lined up behind him. As the red lights of the fire trucks and ambulance approached, I told the officers that the house had not yet been cleared and that it was unknown whether the shooter remained inside. I ordered, "We're gonna make entry to get ourselves between the victim and the threat. Paramedics are on scene and need to get the victim outta here. You guys good?" They both responded without hesitation, "We got you, Sarge. We're good." With no further thought, we made tactical entry to the residence and held our ground as the paramedics worked quickly behind us. As they backed away with the victim in their care and gave the all clear, we began to clear the residence. Broken glass, blood, and personal items were strewn about the residence. There was no one else inside.

From the uniform patrol level, our job was done. We held a secure perimeter as detectives and forensics personnel arrived to the scene. As I reflected on our initial response, it was apparent that none of us were thinking of the danger we faced. Not for a second did we hesitate to place ourselves as human shields before the paramedics. We are public servants. We are brave in the face of adversity. Police and fire personnel alike. We are family. Although the victim did not survive, the responding officers performed flawlessly. It is important to remember that you cannot solve every crime and you cannot save every life. At the end of the day, it is impossible to get those images out of your head. You will carry these things with a heavy soul. But you must remember your support system: your family, your friends, and your brothers and sisters in blue. Law enforcement is a calling. Your brothers and sisters around the world share a common understanding. Keep reading. You're almost there!

- Understanding the interviewers' expectations

- Leaving a lasting impression: Tips and tricks

- Preparing for the most common interview questions

CHAPTER 5

Expect the Unexpected: Interview Prep

POLICE

By NOW, YOU HAVE COMPLETED THE INITIAL APPLICATION, submitted your résumé, and have been in contact with the agency's recruiter. You have had one of two very different experiences: Either the recruiter is on-point and in contact with you on a regular basis, or you have submitted all of your documents and have not heard back from him in weeks. Have no fear. This second situation is normal. Some agencies require frequent contact between the recruiter and the police officer candidates. Other agencies are hands-off and allow the recruiter to conduct business however he sees fit. Many agencies have a disclosure on the application that clearly states, "Do not contact this agency to inquire about the status of your application." That does not necessarily mean you cannot follow up with your contact. You may just need to be strategic about it; be creative, but be cognizant of the appearance you create.

> "...you should dress professionally every time you meet with a representative of the agency"

Remember in Chapter 3 when we discussed the various free online training courses? Well, it may be time to log on and complete one. And when you're done, you might as well stop by the recruiter's office to drop it off. Let him know, "I just completed this course and wanted to know if I could add the certificate to my résumé package." Most likely, you will have triggered the recruiter's thought process, and he will update you as to your status without your having to ask. As previously discussed, you should dress professionally every time you meet with a representative of the agency.

There are several ways to prepare for the big day. Your interview is the bread and butter of the hiring process. It is your opportunity to rise above the other police officer candidates and show that you are the ideal recruit. To begin the preparation, make a list of ten questions that you as an interviewer would ask a fellow police officer candidate. This brainstorming may be difficult, so feel free to enlist a friend or family member for assistance. Sample questions include, but are not limited to, the following:

1. Why do you wish to become a police officer, and how would your appointment benefit this agency?

2. What attracts you to this agency versus another agency?

3. What qualities should a good police officer candidate possess?

4. What are five of your strengths and five of your weaknesses?

5. What can you do to overcome your weaknesses?

6. What would you do if you found out that a fellow police officer was stealing money from the people he arrests?

7. What would you do if you stopped a vehicle for suspected DUI and you found the operator to be your immediate relative (mother, father, brother, sister)?

8. Where do you see yourself in five, ten, and twenty years?

9. How does your family feel about your becoming a police officer?

10. How will you and your family cope with your working extended hours, weekends, midnight shifts, and holidays?

These questions are very basic and very real. The answers you provide should be honest, ethical, and clearly explained. There is no right or wrong answer. The interviewers are not testing your level of intelligence or your allegiance to the badge. They want to hear that you know where your faults are and have a plan to improve them. They want to know that you have the utmost integrity and would not allow a dirty cop to prey on innocent human beings (whether they are criminals or not). They want to know that you are capable of having compassion for others while fulfilling your sworn duty to serve and protect the citizens of the community. And they want to know you can communicate clearly and coherently.

"The simple fact is that police officers must make difficult choices on a regular basis."

Question 7 can be a sticky one. Everyone always asks, "What am I supposed to do? Lock up my mom for DUI?" The legal answer is, "Yes." It does not matter who she is; if she broke the law, she should be arrested like everyone else. The ethical answer is absolutely not. She is your mom; call someone to pick up the car and drive her home. Is that abuse of police discretion? My answer was that I would contact my supervisor, advise him or her of the situation, and indicate that I could not be involved in whatever law enforcement action was or was not taken due to the conflict of interest. You must understand that no one is above the law. I never had the opportunity to ask the interview panel if my answer was acceptable. The simple fact is that police officers must make difficult choices on a regular basis. The privilege of police discretion can bring a lot of trouble when used only intermittently. Integrity is the single most important quality of anyone in law enforcement. Without it, you cannot be trusted by the public or the agency and you cannot testify in court.

> **"Integrity is the single most important quality of anyone in law enforcement."**

Now that you have a general idea of what to expect during the interview, you need to prepare for it. Ask your friends, family, and even any police officers whom you might already know to ask you some interview questions and then to ask you additional questions about the initial answers you provide. Here's another good trick: Try to find out how many people will be on the interview panel. Remember the presentation portfolio we discussed in Chapter 3 containing your résumé, cover letter, and supporting documents (diplomas, degrees, certifications, etc.)? Well, if there are three people on your interview panel, put together four binders. When you arrive, make eye contact and shake the hand of each individual, introduce yourself, and present each of them with a copy of your portfolio. Do not sit down until either the interviewers begin to sit or they invite you to sit first. This strategy may seem a little cliché, but trust me; it creates a good impression. Oh, and by the way, the fourth binder is for you. It is a visual tool that you can flip through as you discuss your abilities with the interviewers. If they sneak a fourth person in on the panel, go ahead and give that person your copy. You should know what's in there without visual prompting anyway. With the portfolio, you are individualizing yourself from other police officer candidates by providing a unique reminder of who you are when the interviewers reflect on the candidates they interviewed that day. By going a little bit above and beyond the requirements (but not too far), you have set yourself above the rest.

When the interview concludes, remember to stand up, make eye contact, and shake the hand of each interviewer. Address each person by rank and name as you thank him or her. Yes, this means that you must actually remember the interviewers' names when (and if) they tell you at the beginning of the interview. Attention to detail is important in law enforcement. Recall from Chapter 1 that you should always remember the name of the person you are speaking with. It is customary to address an officer by their rank and last name. If you do not remember someone's name, address him or her by rank or simply state while you shake hands, "I'm sorry, I want to pronounce your last name right." (This comment will subconsciously prompt the person to repeat his or her name without your even asking! However, if the name is something simple like Smith or Jones, you might look like a fool asking how to pronounce it. So the best practice is still to remember it the first time around.)

Most likely, you will be greeted again by your recruiter when you exit the interview room. The recruiter will ask you how you felt about the interview. Feel free to make small talk, but do not forget that it is "Yes, sir" and "Yes, ma'am." The last words out of your mouth before you leave should be, "Thank you again. I look forward to hearing from you."

Congratulations, your interview is complete! Next comes your background investigation.

IN SOME STATES, DRIVING A VEHICLE WITHOUT A LICENSE or while your operator's license is suspended will land you in handcuffs and behind bars. In other states, like Virginia, the driver is issued a uniform summons (a traffic ticket), and the vehicle is either towed or removed by a licensed driver.

This story brings us back to my first year on the job. I had completed my field training phase and was released to independent patrol. As I canvassed my assigned patrol area, I observed a traffic backup along the East Washington Street corridor. This is a main stretch of roadway within the urban downtown area. It is heavily traveled during both the daytime and evening hours. Just as the sun began to set and the call volume steadily increased, I found myself sitting in traffic with no end in sight. After a few minutes of waiting for the traffic light ahead, the delay turned to horns honking and citizens waving at me as if something had happened near the upcoming intersection. I remember feeling annoyed because I was on my way to grab a cup of coffee and really did not want to be stuck at a vehicle crash. As I activated my police vehicle's emergency equipment and proceeded safely around the stopped traffic, I picked up the radio mic and called-in the congestion. As soon as I aired my call sign, I broke out in laughter. It happened so quickly that I forgot to release my thumb from the radio button as I blurted out, "You've got to be kidding me right now!"

As I looked ahead, I observed a black male teenager wearing a long white t-shirt with blue jeans and nice, clean, Timberland-style work boots. I was completely caught off guard when I saw that he was sitting on a horse and that the horse was blocking the entire intersection! I quickly gathered my composure and advised dispatch that I would be out on East Washington Street with a traffic incident. As I exited my police vehicle, I shouted, "Dude. Seriously? Get out of the roadway!" The young man said nothing.

Instead, he motioned hastily for me to come closer. Now, growing up near a city, I've seen the mounted patrol working in large crowds. And the first thing they teach you is **do not get too close to the horse**. I told the guy that I was not going any closer and that he needed to move the horse out of the roadway. He promptly responded, "I'm sorry, Officer. She won't move. I don't know why, but she just won't move." I watched, chuckling, as he snapped the reins and kicked the stirrups while the horse just stood there with a blank stare. She obviously had no intention of moving.

I advised him that it was not against the law to ride a horse downtown and curiously asked why he was riding the horse and where he had come from (knowing that the closest horse stables were miles outside of town). Again, he motioned for me to come closer as he leaned toward me and whispered, "I'm not trying to make a scene, sir. But my license is suspended." It took everything I had not to burst out laughing. He had ridden the horse nearly twenty miles from his grandfather's house to visit his girlfriend nearby. It was his first time riding alone, and the horse literally would not budge. Fortunately for the both of us, another officer arrived—one with extensive equine experience. The young man dismounted the horse as the other officer took the reins and led it off the roadway. Traffic began to flow normally, and the crowd slowly dispersed. One unruly citizen stood by and yelled to me that I had "no right to be harassing that boy just for riding a horse." I kindly advised the citizen that I let the young man go on a verbal warning for failing to display a headlight on the horse at nighttime (I was obviously joking!) and continued back to my police car with a smile.

The best part about this job is that you truly cannot make this stuff up. When you arrive for your shift and you hit the streets after roll call, you are at the mercy of the wit of the public. It is the greatest adventure that one could ever ask for. Law enforcement is a serious profession, but the day that you lose your sense of humor is the day you should retire.

- Understanding the polygraph procedures

- Adhering to academy expectations

CHAPTER 6

From Background to Academy:
Be the Total Package

For the most part, your hiring process is complete after the interview. From here, the agency will complete your background investigation and, if applicable, schedule your polygraph examination. (As of this writing, some states—such as Massachusetts—have prohibited polygraph examination for employment purposes.) If you have not done so already, notify all of your references (past and present employers, friends, family, neighbors, etc.) that you have completed the interview process and that an investigator may be contacting them to ask questions about you. It is important that your references are not blindsided by the investigator. Take the opportunity to review your background and credentials with your references so that they have a general knowledge of your qualifications. Do not influence your references as to what they should say to the investigator, but give them the information they need to provide a thorough explanation of why you are the ideal candidate.

The polygraph is not designed to determine fact from fiction but rather to verify the consistency of your responses during the application and interview process. As long as you have been 100 percent honest throughout the process, you will do just fine. Remember, telling 99 percent of the truth (omission) is just as bad as lying, and it will disqualify you from the hiring process. I cannot stress enough that, regardless of your past, you should *be honest.* The worst thing you can do is to compromise your integrity by lying about something that may actually be of no concern to your hiring authorities. The key is consistency. A polygraph is designed to detect deception through a sudden increase or decrease in heart rate, blood pressure, breathing, and sometimes eye movement. Many people exhibit these characteristics merely due to nervousness. However, there are certain functions of the human body that are uncontrollable and display as involuntary indicators of deception.

I have found that the single most common disqualifier related to the polygraph is the candidate's omission of marijuana use or underage alcohol consumption. Although any use or possession of marijuana is a violation of law in most states, the background investigators will certainly consider the circumstances in which the drug was used or possessed. For example, many candidates may have experimented with marijuana in a social setting; this isn't necessarily an automatic disqualifier. Definite disqualifiers include having used marijuana within the past twelve months prior to employment, having used marijuana on a habitual basis, or being deceptive about marijuana use. Similarly, law enforcement employers recognize that most college students under twenty-one have illegally consumed alcohol. The polygraph is not meant to scare you. The employer is simply looking for honesty and consistency in your statements. No matter how much you think that what you're admitting may affect you in the hiring process, just have to tell the truth. You may be surprised by the outcome.

Once you have successfully completed the interview, background, and other preemployment objectives, you will receive a conditional offer of employment letter from the agency. As discussed in chapter four, you should be noticing significant increases in strength and cardiovascular capacity as you progress with your structured workout program. Your energy should be more consistent throughout the day and you should be sleeping better during the night. This conditioning is extremely important to the upcoming police academy experience that awaits you.

Now that you have received your conditional offer of employment, speak with your recruiter to determine when and where you will attend the police academy. There are a few variations depending upon the agency: in-house academies, live-in academies, and regional academies. Many larger agencies employ their own in-house academies attended only by personnel from their agencies. This type of training style is often very effective, but it requires a lot of manpower to comprise a training division of certified instructors. The in-house academy concept allows agency-specific training to include policy and procedure. External academies do not generally instruct on local policy and procedure because there are too many variations in the policies of multiple departments coming together for training. External academies focus more on common law offenses, basic investigations, and patrol procedures. Most academies nowadays have websites designed to provide the incoming recruit with insight as to the format of the coming weeks.

Many state police and federal agencies conduct live-in academies that require recruits to live in barracks or dorms for the duration of training (often seventeen to twenty-nine weeks). The live-in academy usually employs a much more paramilitary-type physical fitness and psychological approach to toughen up the recruits or to wash out those who just cannot handle it.

Other academies focus primarily on the academic side of training. For example, most Florida agencies require that the recruit possess a certificate of completion from an academy approved by the FDLE (Florida Department of Law Enforcement) prior to even applying to a law enforcement agency. To accomplish this, the person would attend an accredited community college and enroll in the appropriate police training program. The course is conducted in a hybrid classroom setting.

A regional academy is usually comprised of a board of directors (mainly the chiefs of police from member jurisdictions). The regional academies operate primarily on an academic platform. Many people believe that the regional academies have the underlying goal of just getting recruits through to graduation since the agencies within the region pay to send them there. It makes sense if you think about it. The chiefs of police do not authorize thousands of dollars per recruit for training just to have the recruits wash out and have to find someone else to fill their spots. The regional academies are a business like any other. If recruits are not passing through, then the chiefs of police will soon stop sending them there. It may not be the most efficient way of employing highly trained police officers, but it happens.

In the regional academy setting, recruits will often continue training following graduation by engaging in the in-house post-academy provided at their respective agencies. While the regional academy focuses on general procedures and common law of the academy's jurisdiction, the post-academy focuses on agency-specific topics like policy and procedure, defensive tactics review, less-lethal instruction (Taser and/or oleoresin capsicum (OC), and ethics.

Regardless of the academy that you attend, you will be required to maintain a clean and pressed uniform, highly polished shoes or boots, appropriate haircut (off the shoulders for females and off the ears for males), and clean-shaven face. (If you have not learned how to iron and steam your clothing, I hope you're a quick learner.) When you do attend the academy, be sure to address all instructors as directed by "ma'am" or "sir" or by their ranks. In short, follow the rules, study for your tests, and work as a team. Policing is not a one-person activity. It requires that a highly-trained and disciplined group of individual officers operate as one to accomplish the task at hand. Congratulations, and welcome to law enforcement.

IT WAS A NORMAL EVENING WITH THE FAMILY. After a home-fixed dinner, my wife and I cleaned up the dishes, and the family was ready for bedtime. My son fell asleep watching TV in our bedroom. Shortly after midnight, I awoke to the text message alert sound of my cell phone. Half asleep, I rolled over and grabbed the phone from the dresser. As my eyes adjusted to the light, I had to read the message a few times to comprehend what it said: "Active shooter. All SWAT units contact dispatch and respond immediately." I told my wife that I had to go and gave her and my son a kiss. Within minutes, I had donned my SWAT uniform, grabbed my tactical bag, and was running lights and sirens on my way to the scene. I contacted the emergency communications center to advise that I was on the air and to request the radio channel assignment. The dispatcher provided a situational brief and directed me to the SWAT staging area. The dispatcher informed me that a seventeen-year-old male had ransacked his grandfather's house, destroyed his personal property, and stolen a firearm with an unknown amount of ammunition. The juvenile was on a rampage and had been running around the downtown area firing shots at vacant vehicles and, eventually, even at responding police officers.

Several police officers had been actively tracking the offender through the neighborhoods, along railroad tracks, and through the woods. The offender's final destination was unknown. Officers' personal accounts later indicated that the offender had fired shots at officers so closely that they could hear the hiss of rounds passing by and striking the stationary rail cars behind them.

Once I arrived on scene at the staging area, the emergency communications center announced that it had received 9-1-1 calls from a citizen. The offender had approached the citizen's home and asked to use the phone. Shortly thereafter, when the citizen became frightened and closed the door, the offender began recklessly firing shots through the front door and windows. The offender then ran off toward a nearby construction yard. As SWAT and K9 officers converged, the offender was nowhere to be seen. A perimeter was set up, and the traffic on an adjacent highway was shut down for safety. I was on the secondary response team. As we geared up to travel from the staging area to the active shooter scene, SWAT members from the primary response team reported visual contact with the offender. He had climbed to the top of a four-story tower and, unfortunately, had an elevated view of our entire team.

As the SWAT members made verbal contact with the offender in an attempt to negotiate his surrender, the offender raised a handgun and opened fire on SWAT officers. One member raised his M4 tactical rifle and returned fire. The offender promptly threw down his handgun from the three-story tower and yelled that he would surrender. The handgun hit the ground, and the magazine ejected upon impact. It was unknown, however, if he had any further weapons, so SWAT officers remained in place at the ready. The secondary response team arrived and began to move into position. A sniper team was positioned in the brush at the wood line. The crisis negotiators had also responded. One of the SWAT team leaders had engaged in conversation with the offender,

who agreed to surrender himself. The support teams remained in place while the juvenile climbed back down the side of the tower at the direction of a SWAT officer. Once on the ground, SWAT members and a K9 team moved in to apprehend the offender without further incident. SWAT members then climbed the tower to ensure that no additional offenders or weapons remained atop.

An evening of chaos ended with no injuries to police or to the offender. The Criminal Investigations Division assumed control of the incident, and all other members of law enforcement returned home safely to their loved ones. At the end of the day, that is the goal: We all go home.

To my future brothers and sisters in blue: Stay alert. Stay alive. Blessed are the peacemakers, for they shall be called the children of God (Matthew 5:9).

- Understanding the investigative nature of social media

- Regulating on- and off-duty behaviors

CHAPTER 7

Networking and Social Media

In the early 2000s, law enforcement agencies began to realize the value of social media in background and criminal investigations. The phenomenon was recognized as MySpace succumbed to the overwhelming popularity of Facebook. Although MySpace was initially created for free advertising and fan-following of local bands, it ultimately became the common arena for self-expression among teens. The social media site was quickly overrun by the introduction of the would-be billion-dollar enterprise, Facebook. When Mark Zuckerberg launched Facebook in February 2004, he never would have imagined its future impact on the way of life worldwide. Facebook began as a social-networking outlet for Harvard University students, but it quickly expanded to more colleges and then, in September 2006, to everyone thirteen or older with a valid e-mail address. From that point forward, the flood gates of Facebook presented opportunities for families and schoolmates to stay in contact, businesses to expand advertising, entrepreneurs and nonprofits to present new ideas, and, of course, the criminal element to prey on the vulnerable Internet users who prominently display their personal lives for the world to see.

According to a Facebook media release in March 2013, there were 1.15 billion user accounts registered worldwide. To put those numbers into perspective, the 2012 US Census reported approximately 314 million people living in the United States. These facts are not only baffling but also essential for you to understand as a police officer candidate. You need to be aware of the privacy settings on your accounts and understand that anything and everything that you post to your social media pages can in some way be viewed by others. Most law enforcement agencies have social media policies in place to protect the integrity of the agency.

In the process of recruiting, many agencies require that a police officer candidate sign a full-disclosure waiver to include usernames for all social media accounts (and the privacy settings you select do not make a bit of difference). Do not be surprised if, while you are sitting for your background interview, the recruiter puts a laptop in front of you and says, "Go ahead and log into your Facebook account for me." You should expect that the recruiter will view your present and previous posts, photos, friends, page likes, posts by others about you, photos of you tagged by others, etc. It is important for you as a potential police officer candidate to have the conversation with your family and friends that you are under strict scrutiny and that even what they believe to be an inside joke may be considered derogatory, explicit, or of bad character. If you use social media, be smart about it; do not post anything that you wouldn't want your mother or the chief of police to see on the nightly news.

Another tip is to know who your friends are. Do not just accept a friend because she is pretty or he is handsome. Law enforcement agencies have full-time cybercrime units dedicated to tracking sexual and financial predators through the social networking websites. If you do not know the person who is requesting your friendship, I strongly advise that you do not accept the request. The last thing that any candidate needs is to be sitting in the hot seat when the background investigator sees a known gang member, drug dealer, sexual predator, or even the investigator's own undercover profile linked as your friend. Be smart and use social networking only for keeping in contact with your real-life friends and family.

> **"...do not post anything that you wouldn't want your mother or the chief of police to see on the nightly news."**

While Facebook, Twitter, and Instagram may be where you connect with friends and family, there are other outlets for professional networking. LinkedIn, for example, is a great social media outlet for those seeking to connect with industry professionals. Often times, you will find officers, detectives, police supervisors, and agency recruiters with LinkedIn profiles. I'm not saying that you should flood the department members with professional networking requests, but it may be beneficial to reach out to a few officers or detectives just so that they know who you are when you finally hit the streets. Keep in mind that, with LinkedIn, you are creating a professional networking profile; do not include connections that would compromise or degrade the positive reputation that you're building.

With new social media and networking outlets surfacing on a regular basis, it is easy to get caught up in the craze. There are great advantages to these portals when you use them properly. For example, they are a great way for military families to share each other's experiences from opposite ends of the globe. These sites are also used for communications between city governments and their citizens. Many police departments have a social media connection to alert the public of crime trends or to ask for assistance with the identification of offenders. Investigators use social media location and time stamps to confirm or refute a suspect's statement; if a suspect claimed to be in one place but posted a status from his or her mobile device in another, they have some explaining to do. Businesses use social media to advertise sales and services and to expand their consumer bases. The fact is, social media exploded at the turn of the twenty-first century and will only continue to be incorporated into our everyday lives.

THE TOUR OF DUTY BEGAN LIKE ANY OTHER. It was 1445 hours and time for B-squad roll call. My call sign was B116 (pronounced "Boy-116"). We listened to the sergeant review the administrative messages for the shift, and then we proceeded to crack jokes at one another. That was the B-squad of 2011. We were all hard-chargers. We led the department in every aspect of drug and warrant arrests, and we were always getting into something. This night, of course, was no different than any other. About three-quarters of the way through the shift, I was conducting a traffic stop and had just made contact with the driver who had pulled off the road into a parking lot. I received his Virginia ID card and vehicle registration. For those who don't know, when a driver hands you an ID card rather than his driver's license, that's an indication that his privilege to operate a vehicle is most likely suspended. Well, sure enough, I returned to my patrol vehicle and ran the driver's status: suspended. Just as I cracked my door to go break the bad news, the deafening priority-one tone pierced through the air.

"Beeeeeep! Ten sixty-one on West Washington Street. Any available unit that can respond. Robbery just occurred and suspect left in victim's vehicle. Any unit that can respond." I was on East Washington Street just a few miles away. I hurried back to the vehicle, handed the driver his ID card and advised, "Hey man, as you already knew, your license is suspended. But today is your lucky day. No ticket. No arrest. I've gotta go, but don't drive, you understand?" He replied, "Are you serious?" Before he finished his sentence, I was gone.

I cannot stress to you how important it is to know your patrol zone. You must own your area of responsibility. You must know the shortcuts, running paths, and hideaways so that you know where to go when there's a criminal on the run. I owned my patrol zone. As I traveled toward the scene, I cut down a few back roads with the assumption that the offender knew that the police would take the most direct route to the scene. The first units on the scene and gathered information from the victim. They relayed information via radio that the offender had violently assaulted an elderly man and stolen his Chevrolet Venture minivan. Sure enough, as I approached the next intersection, I spotted the headlights of the minivan just before they blacked out on a side street in a nearby neighborhood. I quickly pulled around and came up behind the vehicle. As I rounded the corner, the headlights illuminated, the tires spun up dirt, and the driver took off.

I radioed to dispatch that I was in pursuit of the suspect vehicle. One problem: I couldn't get through on the air because everyone on the scene was talking to each other. I followed as the vehicle drove up over sidewalks and increased its speed while recklessly navigating the condensed neighborhood. After about forty seconds went by, I finally got through on the radio. "Boy-one sixteen, vehicle pursuit! Fayette St. onto South Main!" Dispatch cleared the air for emergency traffic only, and it was on. I was not letting this guy out of my sight. The minivan skidded sideways as we left the neighborhood to enter the main roadway. The speeds well exceeded the 25 mph posted speed limit as we raced through the downtown area. As the driver gained distance, another unit was catching up. I instructed the other unit to take the lead and I would handle the radio traffic. He was a rookie at the time. I could tell he was excited. The pursuit totaled just over ten miles and reached speeds in excess of 100 mph on the country highways. Due to the increasing speed, the on-duty lieutenant (watch commander) ordered all units to discontinue the pursuit.

We immediately cut off our emergency equipment and slowed to a safe speed. We continued on the path of the pursuit to make sure that the offender had not crashed or run any innocent citizens off of the roadway. Sure enough, about a mile farther, a utility pole lay across the intersection with the minivan tucked securely underneath it. The driver's door was open and the airbags deployed, but the offender was nowhere to be seen. The minivan was obviously totaled. The live wires were draped across the hood. As units set up a perimeter, the search ensued. A citizen called from a nearby neighborhood to report a suspicious male in jeans and a long shirt who was jogging and kept looking back as if he was hiding from someone. A female officer from my academy class keyed up on the radio advising that she was right around the corner. I was also headed that way. As I approached, I could see her blue lights in the distance. She was getting out of her car and the suspect was fast approaching. I arrived on the scene and quickly jumped from my police vehicle. As I did so, I saw her point her finger at him and I heard her shout, "Hey, hey! Stop! Show me your hands and get on the ground. Do it now!"

Much to my surprise, after a violent assault, robbery, carjacking, and ten-mile vehicle pursuit, he put his hands in the air, got down on his knees, and shouted back, "Yes, ma'am!" And just that quickly, it was over. No fight, no shots fired, no taser deployed. Just good stern verbal commands from an officer with an authoritative presence. The suspect ultimately admitted his involvement and was convicted of several felonies.

Always remember that law enforcement has nothing to with how big and bad you are. It is not about your muscles, your ego, or your attitude. If you present yourself in a professional manner with a command presence, you will always walk a paved road. No one can choose your path but you.

- Congratulations! You're on probation :-)

- Learning to work with different personalities

CHAPTER 8

Harness Your Ability to Learn

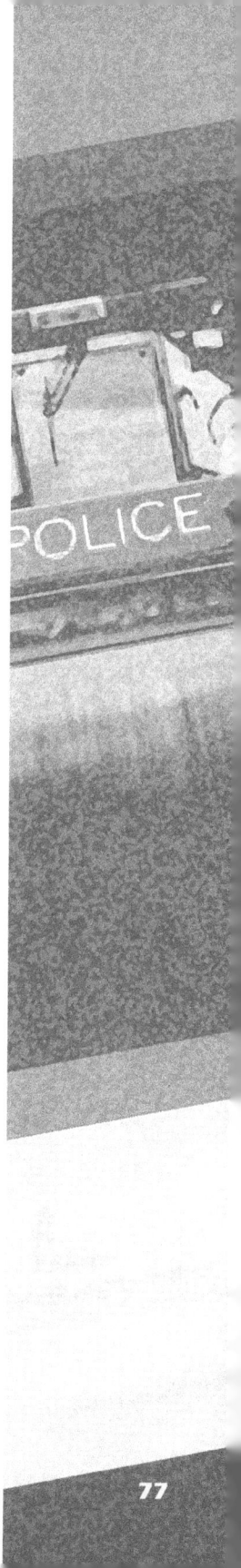

Your primary function as a uniform patrol officer is to answer law enforcement calls for service. Once you have successfully completed the police academy, you will swear your oath as a police officer before your jurisdictional representatives and will receive the badge that you have worked so diligently to earn. In some cases, you will continue to your agency's post-academy training, which usually consists of department, city, or county policy review. Otherwise, you will begin your career in the passenger seat of your field training officer's (FTO's) squad car. Your FTO is, for all intents and purposes, your immediate supervisor during this phase. In decades past, the FTO phase included a fair amount of hazing by the senior officers. As the friendly jokes turned to internal investigations, new policies have restricted such behaviors and, in most cases, made the new officer's initial training phase more enjoyable.

Your FTO is your mentor. You are your FTO's rookie. Do not get upset and become defensive. This is not a time to whine and cry because you feel disrespected. You made the decision in Chapter 1 that you could handle this, remember? There is a difference between hazing and meeting your right of passage. You are a rookie (at least until you have completed the probationary training period). This is the time to ask questions and learn what your department, your peers, and your community expect from you. This is your opportunity to earn the respect of your peers and of the citizens whom you will serve.

You will quickly learn that every officer is a different person with different goals, ethics, and self-determined performance standards. Most agencies nowadays cycle new officers through at least two and sometimes three different FTOs during their training periods for a variety of reasons. Like all human beings, you and your FTO may have personality conflicts that you simply cannot overcome. It does not make sense to put two people in a car for eight hours and expect them to work efficiently for others if they cannot even work together.

The rotation is also important because every person has something new to offer. It is not uncommon for a seasoned field training officer to learn something new from a rookie. You are a new officer, and you may have new ideas and can present an alternative approach to certain things that have been overlooked by the complacency of a senior officer. There are senior officers who will encourage you to jump out with people who appear to be violating a law or city ordinance and to address the violation with appropriate law enforcement action. Other senior officers may tell you to sit there, shut up, and stay in the vehicle unless they say otherwise. Exposure to these varying types of officers will help you to understand who you are and what type of officer you will become.

There was a retired US Navy Chief in my police academy class. He told us that he had been supervising others for nearly twenty years but always wanted to be a cop. I could only imagine the thought process of sitting in the squad car as a rookie again after rising through the ranks with such responsibility. I spoke with him a few weeks after graduation and asked how things were going. He said, "Man, I love this stuff. I come to work, somebody [his FTO] tells me where I need to be and what I need to do, and I don't have to worry about making sure someone else is doing his job." There was another person in my class who made it clear that no one could tell him what to do. He is no longer employed in law enforcement.

"Align yourself with positive role models and you will become a positive role model for others."

Your field training phase is the foundation for defining who you will become as a police officer. Your attitude, whether positive or negative, will certainly influence those around you. When you arrive at the scene of an incident, and you present yourself in a courteous and professional manner, the citizens will more than likely comply with your requests. On the contrary, when you belittle people and act as if you could care less about their problems, you will be greeted with criticism and tension. It won't take long for you to learn which officers break up fights and which officers tend to cause them. Align yourself with positive role models and you will become a positive role model for others.

There is nothing more rewarding than a career in law enforcement. To take a dangerous drug dealer or a habitual thief off the streets, to mentor a child who has little or no guidance at home, or to realize tearfully when you look in the mirror after your shift that you saved a life today—there is nothing like it.

- Exploring every opportunity

- Navigating detours

- Remembering where you came from and your experiences will help to pave the path for others

CHAPTER 9

Focus on Today, but Know Your Path May Change Tomorrow

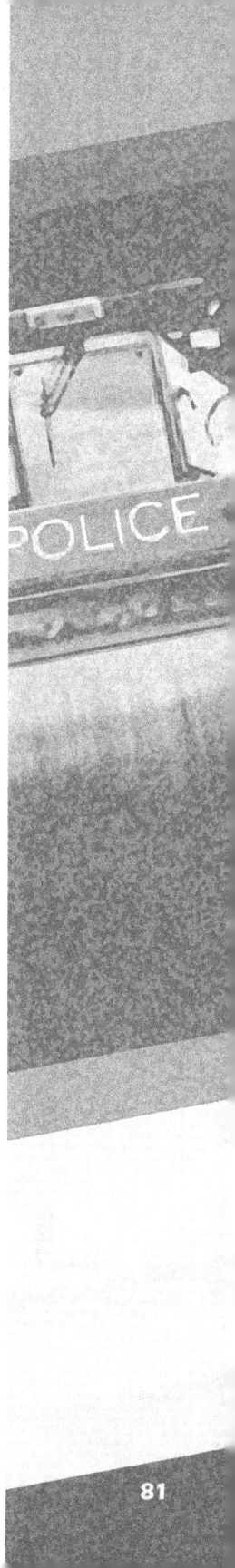

Success is the ability to understand that there is always something else to learn and to improve upon. In the first few chapters, you made some decisions as to where your path to policing may lead you. It is also important to know that no unbeaten path is laid in a straight line. There will be forks in the road along the way. You may intend to go right, but an unexpected obstacle forces you left. I chose only to apply to law enforcement agencies with a K9 program. Well, over the three years it took me to write this book, my path to policing has changed. I participated in the K9 hiring process in 2011, but did not meet the time in service requirements at the time of the position posting. Shortly thereafter, the department posted a position for criminal investigations (detective). I applied for the position and participated in the interview process. I was ranked number one on the eligibility list and earned the rank of detective in 2011. I was placed on a training rotation and cycled through the criminal investigations FTO process. Upon completion, I was a general assignment detective under the Property Crimes section. I have since had assignments to the Burglary Unit and Economic Crimes Unit. I had the opportunity to train new detectives and to mentor uniform patrol officers who aspired to become detectives. I participated in the selection process and was appointed to my department's SWAT team. I completed a basic SWAT school and remained active on the team for more than a year. All the while, I had not given up on my dream of becoming a K9 handler. My supervisors and peers were well aware that if there was another posting for the K9 Unit, I would be applying.

There is a turning point in every officer's career where he or she must make a decision. My initial path was directed toward the K9 program. However, my career had advanced to such a level of knowledge and understanding, I felt that I'd be stepping back if I were to return to uniform patrol as a K9 handler. I had to decide whether to stick to my dream of working a police dog or to take the promotional test for the rank of sergeant, where my training, education, and experience would prove to be an asset to my peers and the department. It was not a decision I was yet prepared to make. I elected to let time decide for me. I would wait for the K9 posting, and if it did not come up before the next promotional exam, then I would take the test to become a sergeant.

I participated in the promotional testing process for the rank of sergeant in 2014. I completed the process, finished among the top three candidates, and was promoted September 1, 2014. As I look back at my achievements thus far in my career, I can no longer see the dirt path on which I began. As I look forward, I see a paved road with no end in sight. The opportunities in law enforcement are endless. Your path will only lead you to where you are willing to follow it. I look forward to the privilege of leadership. Good leaders remain optimistic. Great leaders learn from those they lead. I urge you to remain vigilant. I encourage you to continue to learn and to teach. As I continue on my path, I will document my journey and look forward to guiding you through yours. I remind you to focus on today, but know your path may change tomorrow. I pray for the safety of you and your squad mates. I encourage you to leave work at the door when you get home, and leave home at the door when you get to work. Be smart, be alert, and stay alive. You have chosen a profession desired by many and earned by only the best. As you don the badge of honor, remember where you came from. Remember that you are not above the law. You are a person of positive morals and utmost integrity. Congratulations, welcome, and good luck!

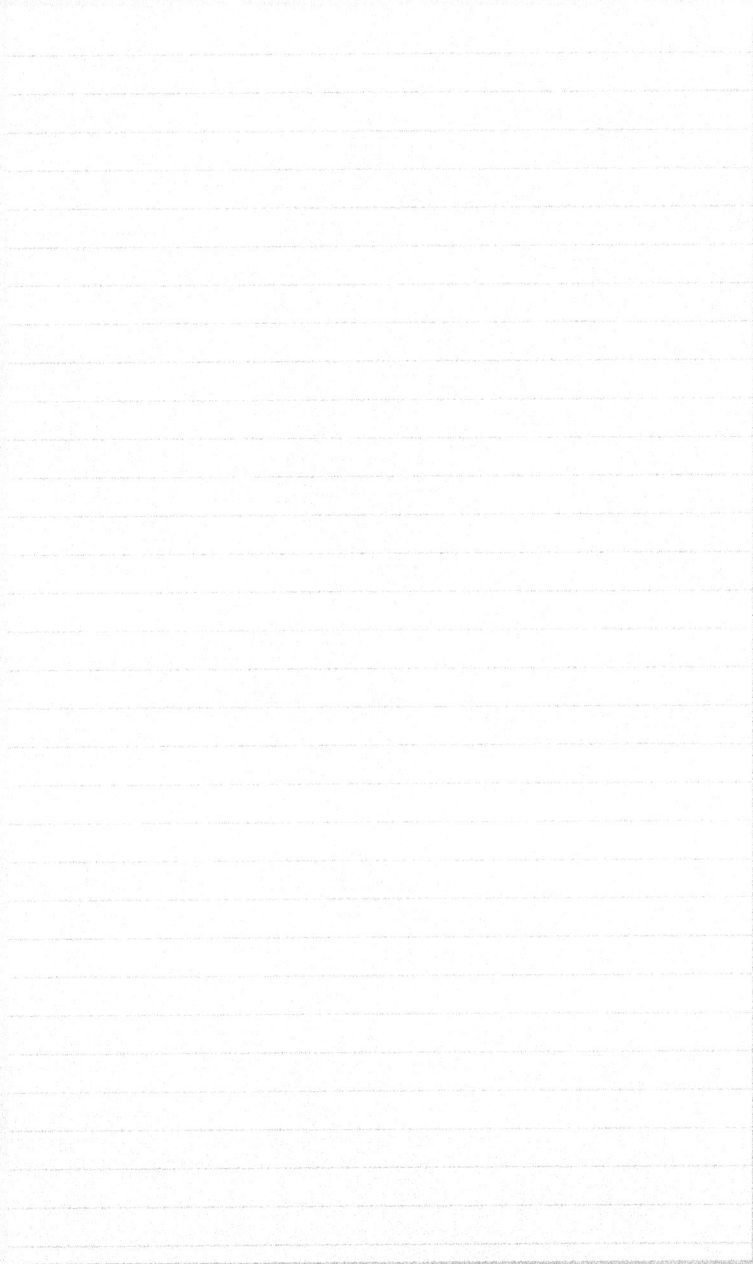

Stay tuned...

More to come on
leadership, supervision,
and other professional topics

from Jeffrey H. Lurie

PAVING
YOUR PATH
PUBLISHING

Check out our website at at
www.pavingyourpath.com

PAVING YOUR PATH
PUBLISHING

www.ingramcontent.com/pod-product-compliance
Lightning Source LLC
Chambersburg PA
CBHW071528200326
41519CB00019B/6112